Shoe Box Math
Learning Centers

40 Easy-to-Make, Fun-to-Use Centers
With Instant Reproducibles and Activities That Help
Kids Practice Important Math Skills Independently!

by Jacqueline Clarke

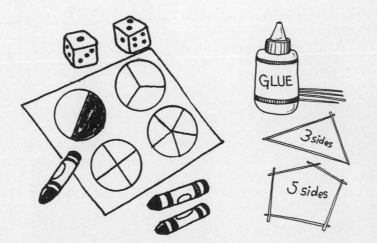

SCHOLASTIC
PROFESSIONAL BOOKS

New York • Toronto • London • Auckland • Sydney
Mexico City • New Delhi • Hong Kong • Buenos Aires

For Garrett, who used his
"together time" to help with the book.

Acknowledgements:
Deborah Schecter—thank you
for your patience!

Cover design by Pamela Simmons

Cover photos by Donnelly Marks

Interior design by Sydney Wright

Interior art by Maxie Chambliss

ISBN: 0-439-20574-3

Contents

Introduction

What is *Shoe Box Math*?

Shoe Box Math allows you to create 40 engaging hands-on math centers using inexpensive and readily available materials. Each center fits neatly inside a shoe box and can be assembled ahead of time, pulled out as needed, and stored conveniently when not in use!

These centers provide children with a concrete way to practice and reinforce the math concepts you teach. Most are open-ended, which allows children to repeat the activity several times until center time is through.

Why use centers in math?

One of the greatest benefits of using centers in math is that it provides teachers with the opportunity to work with small groups or individuals. This time can be used to introduce a new concept, assess children's progress, or provide individual assistance to a struggling child.

While working at a center, children not only benefit from the math task at hand, but also learn skills such as cooperation, time management, accountability, and responsibility for materials.

How to use *Shoe Box Math*

The games and activities in *Shoe Box Math* were designed to be used by small groups of three or four students at centers, but can easily be adapted for whole class lessons or one-on-one teaching.

If you have already included a math station as one of your centers, *Shoe Box Math* will work well with what you've already established. Another option is to use the activities during your "math time" in conjunction with other math centers such as computers, pencil and paper, and small group instruction. In the latter case, children can visit one to four centers per day, depending upon your schedule. Here is a suggested weekly plan for a 40-minute block of time:

	Monday	Tuesday	Wednesday	Thursday	Friday
20 min.	Whole Group	Whole Group	Whole Group	Whole Group	Open
20 min.	Centers	Centers	Centers	Centers	Open

Using this weekly plan, the class is divided into four groups, with each group visiting one center per day (small group, *Shoe Box Math*, pencil and paper, or computers). When children finish their center work, they may choose to play a math game until center time is over. The "open" time scheduled for Friday may be used to introduce a new concept, teach an interdisciplinary math lesson, or read math-related literature.

How is *Shoe Box Math* organized?

There are three centers for each area of your math curriculum. Copy each page onto colored paper (or have children decorate), cut along the lines, and glue onto a shoe box to create the center. Each center includes:

- **Title and Directions.** The title becomes the box label—simply glue it to one side of the shoe box for easy storage and retrieval. Cut out the directions and glue to the inside lid of the shoe box.

- **Reproducible Pages.** Record sheets, math mats, game boards, and patterns are just some of the reproducibles you'll include in the centers.

- **Materials.** Check here to find out which items you'll need for each center. Most materials can be found in your home or classroom.

- **Putting It Together.** Here's where you'll find simple directions to assemble each center. In most cases, all you'll need to do is gather materials and make copies of the reproducibles.

- **Tips** and **Beyond the Center** provide helpful hints and extension activities.

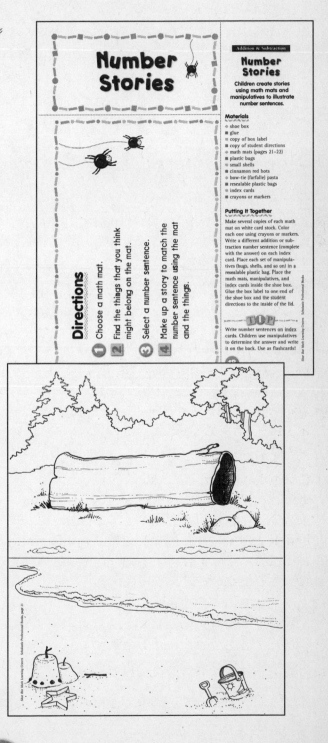

Meeting the NCTM Standards

	Numbers and Operation	Estimation*	Numbers Sense and Numeration*	Concepts of Whole Number Operation*	Whole Number Computation*	Fractions and Decimals	Patterns, Functions and Algebra	Geometry and Spatial Sense	Measurement	Data Analysis, Statistics and Probability	Problem Solving	Reasoning and Proof	Communication	Connections	Representation
Numbers & Counting	●		●	●	●						●	●	●	●	●
Numeral Writing	●		●								●	●	●	●	●
Addition & Subtraction	●			●	●						●	●	●	●	●
Place Value	●		●	●	●						●	●	●	●	●
Geometry	●		●				●	●			●	●	●	●	●
Sorting & Classifying	●						●				●	●	●	●	●
Patterning	●						●				●	●	●	●	●
Multiplication	●		●	●	●						●	●	●	●	●
Probability	●									●	●	●	●	●	●
Time	●		●						●		●	●	●	●	●
Measurement	●	●	●						●	●	●	●	●	●	●
Money	●		●								●	●	●	●	●
Fractions	●		●			●			●		●	●	●	●	●

* Indicates a subcategory of Numbers and Operation

Race to 100

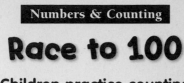

Race to 100

Children practice counting to 100 as they race to color in all the squares on a hundred board.

Materials

- shoe box
- glue stick
- copy of student directions
- copy of box label
- hundred board (page 10)
- crayons
- two number cubes

Putting It Together

Make several copies of the hundred board. Place the hundred boards, crayons, and number cubes inside the shoe box. Glue the box label to one end of the shoe box and the student directions to the inside of the lid.

Directions (for 2 or more players)

1. Take turns rolling the number cubes and adding together the two numbers you rolled.

2. Color in that total number of squares on your hundred board. Work in number order.

3. The first player to color in all of the squares wins the game!

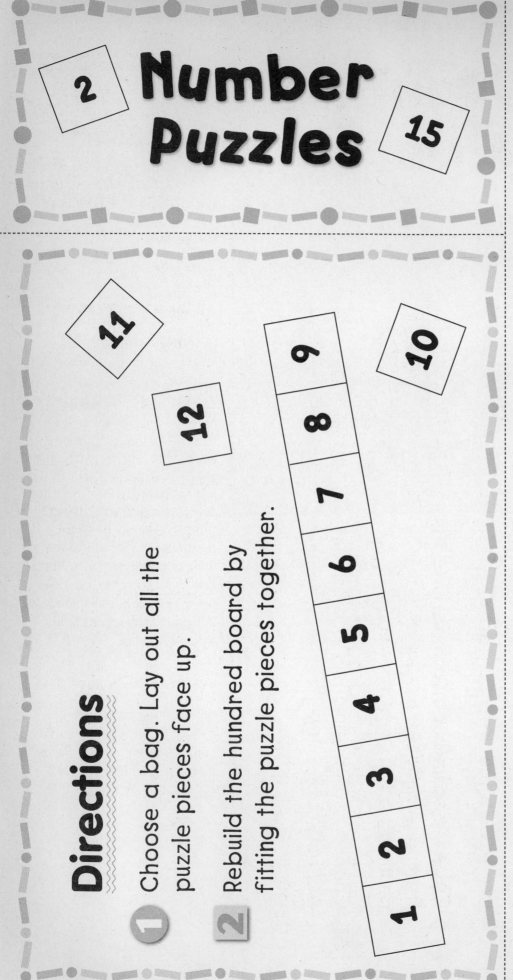

Number Puzzles

2 **15**

11 **12** **10**

9 8 7 6 5 4 3 2 1

Directions

1. Choose a bag. Lay out all the puzzle pieces face up.

2. Rebuild the hundred board by fitting the puzzle pieces together.

Number Puzzles

Using their knowledge of the number system, children reconstruct hundred board puzzles.

Materials

- shoe box
- glue
- copy of student directions
- copy of box label
- hundred board (page 10)
- sturdy paper
- several large resealable bags

Putting It Together

Copy several hundred boards onto sturdy paper (you might even laminate them) and cut along the lines. Put each set inside a plastic bag and place the bags inside the shoe box. Glue the box label to one end of the shoe box and the student directions to the inside of the lid.

TIP

Depending on students' levels, you can cut apart the hundred board in different ways: rows, single numbers, or random "chunks."

Skip-Counting Strips

Skip-Counting Strips

Children create a frieze to illustrate counting by 2's, 3's, 4's, or 5's.

Materials

- shoe box
- glue
- copy of student directions
- copy of box label
- adding machine tape
- several copies of hundred board (page 10)
- patterns (10 copies, page 11)
- crayons
- scissors

Putting It Together

Make copies of patterns and hundred boards. Place the patterns, crayons, glue, and adding machine tape inside the shoe box. Glue the box label to one end of the shoe box and the student directions to the inside of the lid.

Beyond the Center

Children can make two handprints on one sheet of paper. Arrange all the papers in a row to create a frieze for counting by 10's.

Directions

1. Color every other square on your hundred board to show the pattern for counting by 2's (start with the number 2).

2. Cut out ten ice cream cones. Glue them in a row to the strip of paper.

3. Copy the number pattern (2, 4, 6, 8) from your hundred board onto the cones. Read the pattern aloud.

4. Choose another counting pattern (by 3's, 4's, or 5's) and repeat with the cakes, flowers, or hands.

Hundred Board

1	2	3	4	5	6	7	8	9	10
11	12	13	14	15	16	17	18	19	20
21	22	23	24	25	26	27	28	29	30
31	32	33	34	35	36	37	38	39	40
41	42	43	44	45	46	47	48	49	50
51	52	53	54	55	56	57	58	59	60
61	62	63	64	65	66	67	68	69	70
71	72	73	74	75	76	77	78	79	80
81	82	83	84	85	86	87	88	89	90
91	92	93	94	95	96	97	98	99	100

Skip-Counting Patterns

4 Finger Writing 0

Finger Writing

Children use fun tactile surfaces to practice numeral writing.

Materials

- shoe box
- glue
- copy of student directions
- copy of box label
- several large resealable bags
- finger paint, hair gel (can be tinted with food coloring), or shaving cream
- one set of numeral cards (pages 15–17)

Putting It Together

Fill bags half full with paint, hair gel, or shaving cream, squeeze out excess air, and seal. Copy the numeral cards onto card stock and cut them out. Place the cards and bags inside the shoe box. Glue the box label to one end of the shoe box and the student directions to the inside of the lid.

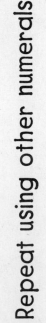

Directions

1 Choose a bag and a numeral card.

2 Place the numeral card under the bag and trace over it using your finger or the eraser end of a pencil.

3 Repeat using other numerals.

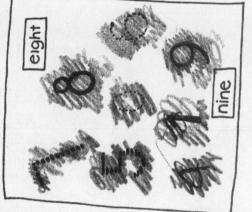

Directions

1. Choose a numeral and place it under your paper.

2. Use the crayons to make a rubbing of the numeral.

3. Continue with other numerals to create a collage. Glue the number words next to their numerals.

Number Collages

Children create and display collages from crayon rubbings of textured numerals.

Materials
~~~~~~~~~~

- shoe box
- glue
- copy of student directions
- copy of box label
- sandpaper
- corrugated cardboard
- colored glue
- scissors
- one set of numeral and number word cards (pages 15–17)
- crayons
- several sheets of white paper

Putting It Together
~~~~~~~~~~

To make textured numerals, cut out numeral shapes from sandpaper and corrugated cardboard. Make a third set by tracing the numerals on the numeral cards with colored glue and let dry. Place the three sets of textured numerals, crayons, and paper inside the shoe box. Glue the box label to one end of the shoe box and the student directions to the inside of the lid.

Playdough Numerals

Directions

1. Choose a numeral card.

2. Roll the playdough into a thin "snake" and use it to form the numeral on the card.

3. Continue until you have a full set of numerals from 1 to 10. Arrange them in a row in order.

Playdough Numerals

Children bend and shape playdough to form numerals.

Materials

- shoe box
- glue
- copy of student directions
- copy of box label
- non-hardening playdough
- one set of numeral cards (pages 15–17)

Putting It Together

Copy the numeral cards onto card stock, cut them out and laminate. Place the cards and playdough inside the shoe box. Glue the box label to one end of the shoe box and the student directions to the inside of the lid.

one	two
three	four
five	six
seven	eight
nine	ten

Number Stories

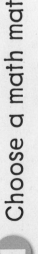

Directions

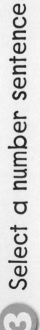

1. Choose a math mat.

2. Find the things that you think might belong on the mat.

3. Select a number sentence.

4. Make up a story to match the number sentence using the mat and the things.

Number Stories

Children create stories using math mats and manipulatives to illustrate number sentences.

Materials

- shoe box
- glue
- copy of box label
- copy of student directions
- math mats (pages 21–22)
- plastic bugs
- small shells
- cinnamon red hots
- bow-tie (farfalle) pasta
- resealable plastic bags
- index cards
- crayons or markers

Putting It Together

Make several copies of each math mat on white card stock. Color each one using crayons or markers. Write a different addition or subtraction number sentence (complete with the answer) on each index card. Place each set of manipulatives (bugs, shells, and so on) in a resealable plastic bag. Place the math mats, manipulatives, and index cards inside the shoe box. Glue the box label to one end of the shoe box and the student directions to the inside of the lid.

Write number sentences on index cards. Children use manipulatives to determine the answer and write it on the back. Use as flashcards!

Button Bags

Directions

1. Choose a number card and put that number of buttons into the bag. Seal the bag.

2. Move the buttons to either side of the line to create a number combination and write that number sentence on a sheet of paper.

3. Move the buttons again to make and write as many different number sentences as you can.

Button Bags

Children manipulate buttons inside a plastic bag to create different combinations for the same number.

Materials

- shoe box
- glue
- copy of student directions
- copy of box label
- medium-sized resealable plastic bags
- 10 buttons
- permanent marker
- nine index cards
- paper and pencil

Putting It Together

Use the marker to draw one line do. n the center of each plastic bag (so that the bag is divided in half). Write a number between 2 and 10 on index cards. Place the bags, cards, buttons, and paper inside the shoe box. Glue the box label to one end of the shoe box and the student directions to the inside of the lid.

Domino Facts

Domino Facts

$$5 + 3 = 8$$
$$5 - 3 = 2$$

$$4 + 1 = 5$$
$$4 - 1 = 3$$

$$3 + 2 = 5$$
$$3 - 2 = 1$$

Directions

1. Choose a domino and place it on the shape on the record sheet.

2. Use the two numbers made by the dots to make number sentences (one addition, one subtraction) on the lines.

3. Remove the domino and draw its dots. Repeat using other dominoes.

Domino Facts

Children use dominoes to record addition and subtraction number sentences.

Materials

- shoe box
- glue
- copy of student directions
- copy of box label
- set of dominoes
- several record sheets (page 23)

Putting It Together

Make several copies of the record sheet. Place the record sheets and dominoes inside the shoe box. Glue the box label to one end of the shoe box and the student directions to the inside of the lid.

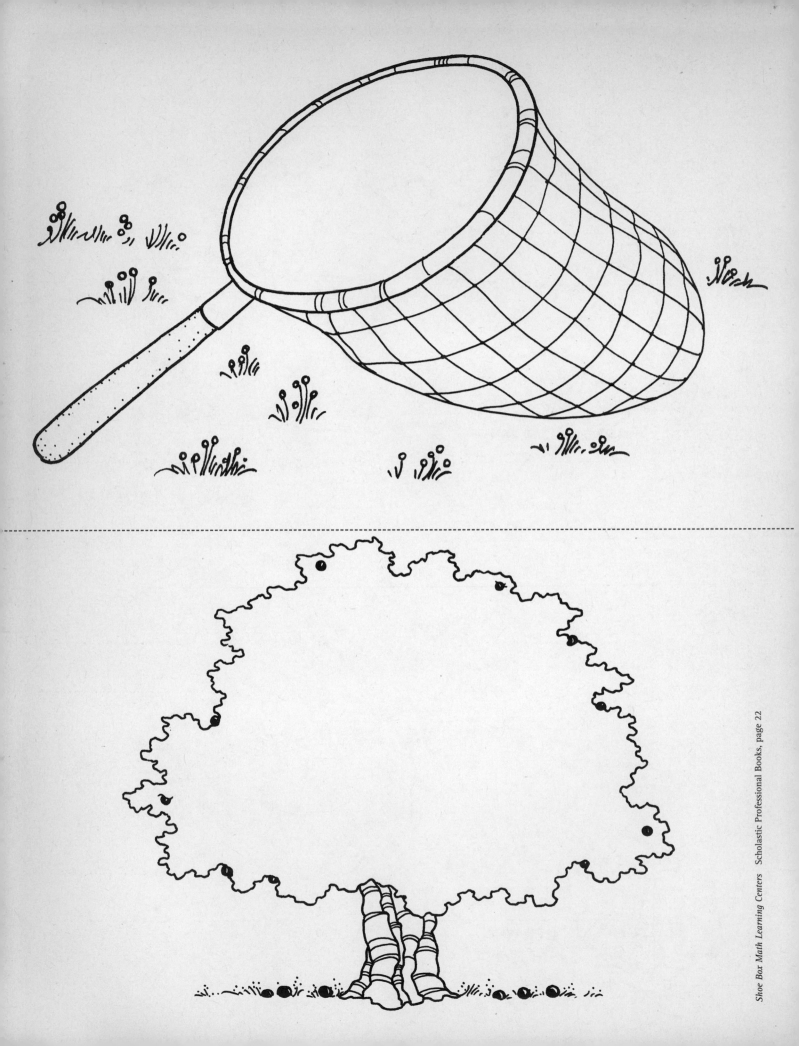

Domino Facts

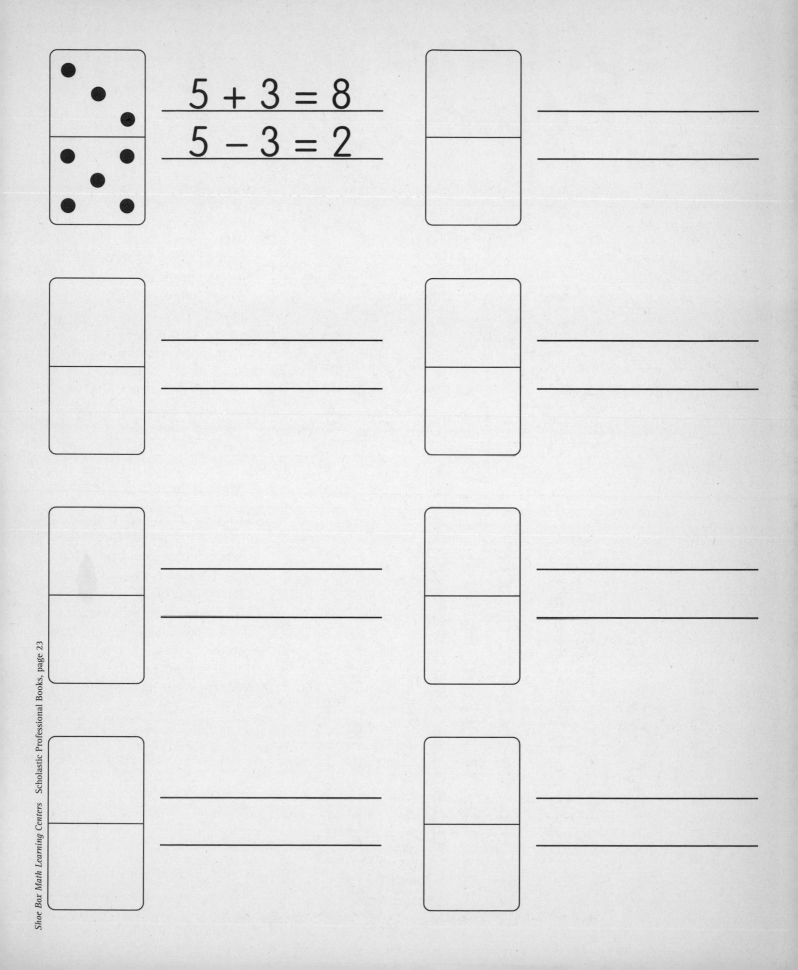

5 + 3 = 8
5 − 3 = 2

Spill and Count

Tens	Ones
2	3

Directions

1. Choose a bag.

2. Count out the objects in your bag onto the ten frames.

3. Count the total number using the ten frames. Write the number in tens and ones on the record sheet.

4. Choose a new bag of objects and repeat.

Spill and Count

Children count out two-digit amounts using ten frames.

Materials

- shoe box
- glue
- copy of student directions
- copy of box label
- 10 ten frames (5 copies of page 27)
- several record sheets (page 28)
- 10 large resealable plastic bags
- small objects in random amounts under 100 (such as 56 beans, 34 pieces of popcorn, 18 paper clips, 64 buttons, 22 stones, 70 pennies, and so on)

Putting It Together

Place each set of objects in a resealable plastic bag (keep objects separate). Label each bag with a number between 1 and 10. Make several copies of the record sheet. Place the bags, ten frames, and record sheets inside the shoe box. Glue the box label to one end of the shoe box and the student directions to the inside of the lid.

Shoe Box Math Learning Centers Scholastic Professional Books

Roll the Biggest Number

Directions (for 2 or more players)

1. Take turns rolling the number cube and writing the number you rolled in the hundred's place. On your second turn, write the number you rolled in the ten's place. On your third turn, write the number you rolled in the one's place.

2. When all three place holders have been filled, read the whole number aloud.

3. The player with the largest number wins the game!

Roll the Biggest Number

Game Number	Hundreds	Tens	Ones	Game Number	Hundreds	Tens	Ones
1	7	2	4	6			
2	2	6	8	7			
3	4	2	7	8			
4	9	5	1	9			
5				10			

Roll the Biggest Number

Children build three-digit numbers by rolling number cubes and recording numerals in the hundred's, ten's, and one's place.

Materials

- shoe box
- glue
- copy of student directions
- copy of box label
- number cube
- game board (page 28)

Putting It Together

Make several copies of the game board. Place the game boards and number cubes inside the shoe box. Glue the box label to one end of the shoe box and the student directions to the inside of the lid.

Vary the game so that the player who creates the smallest number wins. Or, let children choose which place to write each number in.

Spin and Show

Directions

1. Place the top in the center of the hundred board and spin.

2. Wait for it to stop and then read the number.

3. Create that number using the beans and ten frames (put 10 beans in each square).

Spin and Show

Children use a toy top to "spin" a number and then represent it using beans and ten frames.

Materials

- shoe box
- glue
- copy of student directions
- copy of box label
- hundred board (page 10)
- several ten frames (page 27)
- dried beans in self-sealing bag
- toy top

Putting It Together

Make copies of the hundred board and ten frames. Place the hundred board, ten frames, beans, and toy top inside the shoe box. Glue the box label to one end of the shoe box and the student directions to the inside of the lid.

If space allows, use four hundred boards to make one giant board!

Ten Frame

Ten Frame

Spill-and-Count Record Sheet

Bag Number	Tens	Ones	Bag Number	Tens	Ones
1			6		
2			7		
3			8		
4			9		
5			10		

Roll the Biggest Number

Game Number	Hundreds	Tens	Ones	Game Number	Hundreds	Tens	Ones
1				6			
2				7			
3				8			
4				9			
5				10			

What's in a Shape?

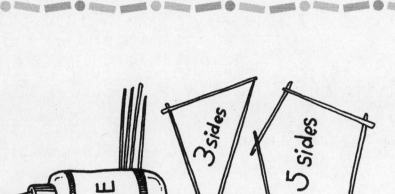

Children count and record the number of sides and corners found on shapes created from toothpicks.

Materials

- shoe box
- glue
- copy of box label
- copy of student directions
- box of toothpicks
- record sheet (page 33)

Putting It Together

Make several copies of the record sheet. Place the record sheets, glue, and toothpicks inside the shoe box. Glue the box label to one end of the shoe box and the student directions to the inside of the lid.

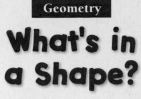

Cotton swabs or straws cut in thirds may be substituted for toothpicks.

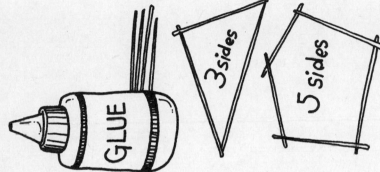

Directions

1. Use the toothpicks to create closed shapes.

2. Glue each shape onto your record sheet.

3. Count and write the number of sides and corners found on each shape.

4. Describe the shape you made.

Shape Museum

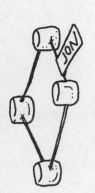
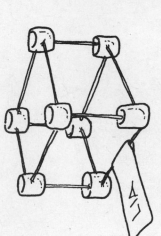

Shape Museum

Children create a "museum" of 3-D shapes from toothpicks and marshmallows and discuss the properties of each shape.

Materials

- shoe box
- glue
- copy of student directions
- copy of box label
- box of toothpicks
- mini-marshmallows in self-sealing bags
- masking tape

Putting It Together

Place the toothpicks, marshmallows, and masking tape inside the shoe box. Glue the box label to one end of the shoe box and the student directions to the inside of the lid. Set aside table space for children to display their structures when finished.

Beyond the Center

Gather children around the "museum." Let them take turns describing the shapes they've created. Help them to identify the type of shape(s) used in their structure and to count the numbers of sides, corners, and faces.

Marshmallows are easier to work with if they have been left out overnight.

Directions

1. Create different shapes using toothpicks and marshmallows.

2. Write your name on a piece of masking tape and put it on your shapes.

3. Display your shapes at the "shape museum."

Color Symmetry

Directions

1 Choose a shape.

2 Color in the squares and parts of squares on one side of the shape using different colored crayons.

3 Make the two sides symmetrical— the same on both sides— by copying the color pattern onto the other side of the shape.

Color Symmetry

Given various shapes, children color symmetrical designs and patterns.

Materials

- shoe box
- glue
- copy of student directions
- copy of box label
- symmetrical shapes (page 32)
- crayons
- scissors

Putting It Together

Make several copies of the symmetrical shapes. Cut out each one separately along the outer solid lines. Place the shapes and crayons inside the shoe box. Glue the box label to one end of the shoe box and the student directions to the inside of the lid.

Beyond the Center

Use the shapes the children have colored to create symmetrical puzzles. Cut each shape in half and let children try to match the two sides.

Color Symmetry

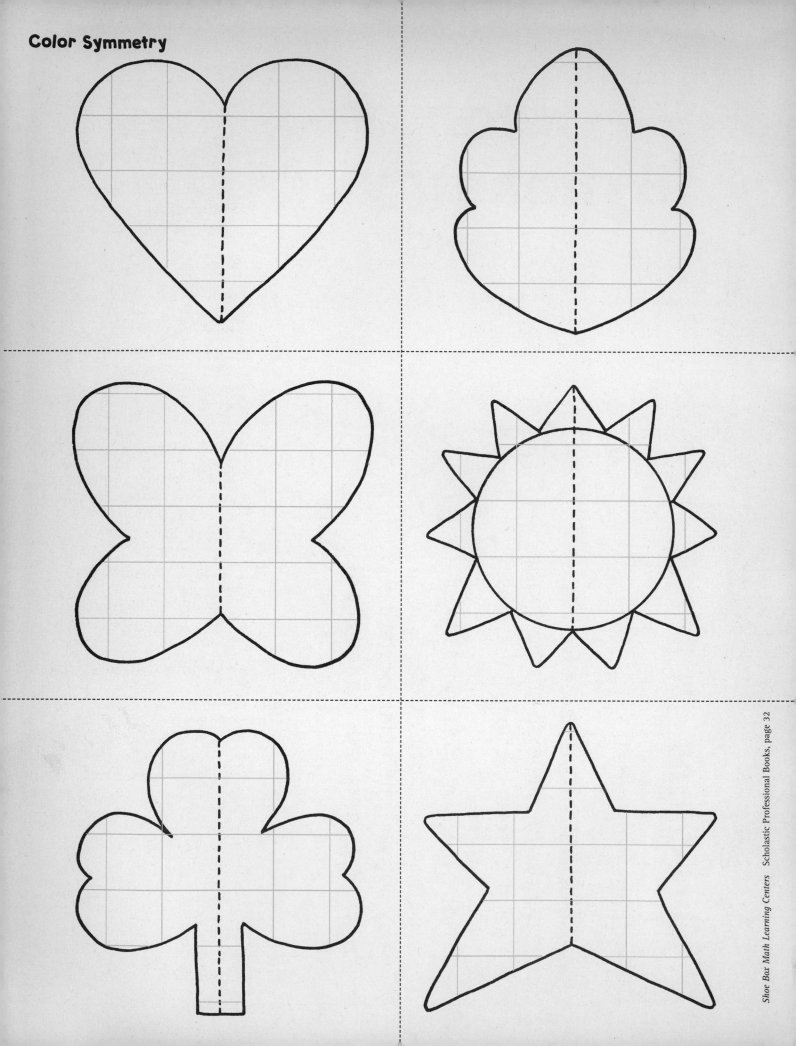

Name _____ Date _____

What's in a Shape?

My shape has _____ sides and _____ corners.

It looks like _____ .

The Attribute Chain

The Attribute Chain

Similar to dominoes, this game invites children to create a row of objects by matching attributes.

Materials

- shoe box
- glue
- copy of student directions
- copy of box label
- assortment of small objects in different shapes, sizes, and colors (toy cars, cereal, buttons, blocks, plastic animals, letter tiles, and so on) in self-sealing bags

Putting It Together

Place the objects inside the shoe box. Glue the box label to one end of the shoe box and the student directions to the inside of the lid.

Model an attribute chain for the group before children work independently. For instance, in the picture on the direction sheet, the chain is "round," "round button," "button," "round letter on square tile," and "square bolt."

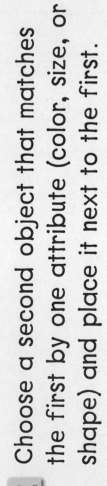

Directions

1. Choose one object from the box and place it on the floor or table.

2. Choose a second object that matches the first by one attribute (color, size, or shape) and place it next to the first.

3. Keep choosing and matching objects, making a long chain, until no more matches can be made. Repeat with a new object.

Class Photo Sort

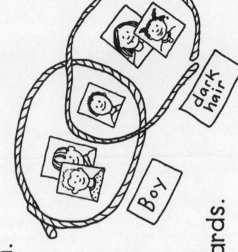

Directions

1. Create a Venn diagram with the yarn.

2. Put the index cards facedown. Choose two and place one under each circle.

3. Sort the photos into groups according to the words written on the index cards. Repeat with different index cards.

Shoe Box Math Learning Centers   Scholastic Professional Books

Class Photo Sort

Children sort classmates' photos using a Venn diagram.

Materials

- shoe box
- glue
- copy of student directions
- copy of box label
- photo of each student
- yarn
- scissors
- index cards
- marker

Putting It Together

Cut yarn into two 36-inch strands. Copy the following words onto separate index cards: boy, girl, blond hair, red hair, dark hair, blue eyes, brown eyes, black eyes, green eyes. Place the photos, strips of yarn, and index cards inside the shoe box. Glue the box label to one end of the shoe box and the student directions to the inside of the lid.

Cereal Sort

Cereal Sort

Challenge children to find different ways to sort cereal.

Materials

- shoe box
- glue
- copy of student directions
- copy of box label
- cereal in various shapes, sizes, and colors
- several copies of sorting mats (page 37)
- blank paper
- self-sealing bags

Putting It Together

Place the mats, paper, and cereal inside the shoe box. Glue the box label to one end of the shoe box and the student directions to the inside of the lid.

Beyond the Center

How many different "sorting rules" did children use to sort the cereal? Make a list of the strategies children used. Use the chart as a resource when sorting other objects.

Directions

1 Think about how you might sort the cereal. Sort the cereal using the sorting mats.

2 How did you decide how to sort? Record your sorting rule on a piece of paper.

3 Repeat. How many sorting rules can you list?

Shoe Box Math Learning Centers Scholastic Professional Books

Cereal Sort

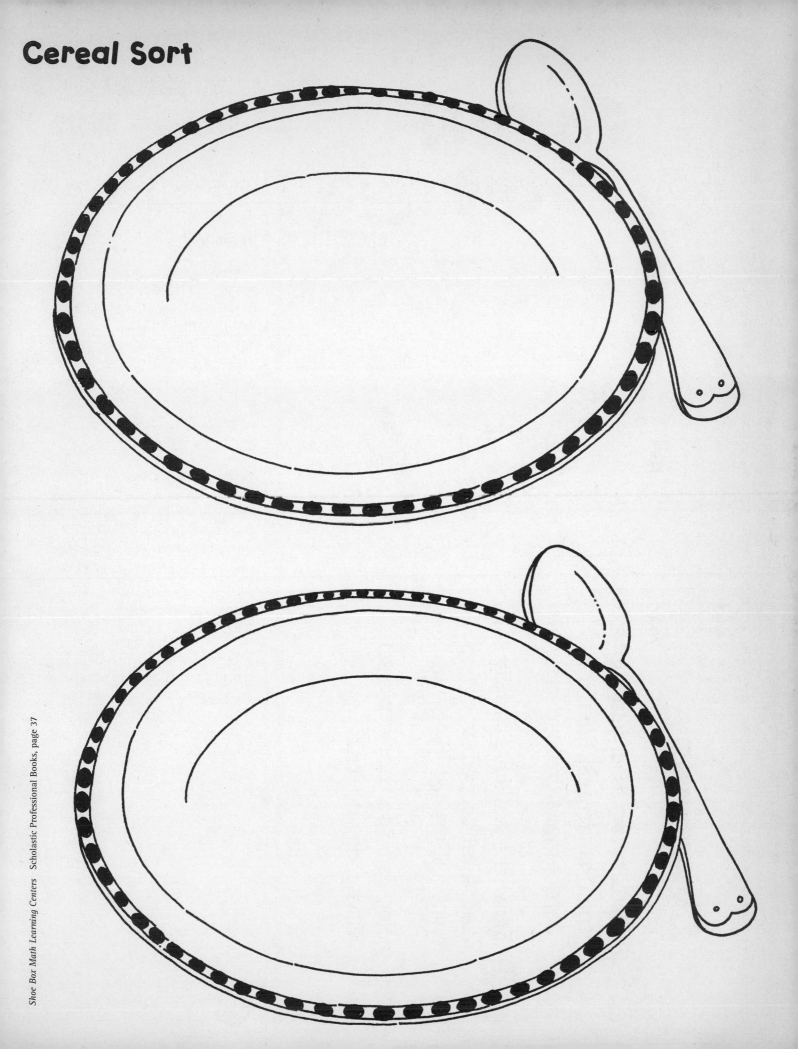

Pattern Pals

Pattern Pals

Using fabric pieces of their own design, children create patterned fashions!

Materials

- shoe box
- glue
- copy of student directions
- copy of box label
- fabric templates (page 41)
- blank paper
- crayons

Putting It Together

Make several copies of the fabric templates. Place the fabric templates, crayons, scissors, glue, and paper inside the shoe box. Glue the box label to one end of the shoe box and the student directions to the inside of the lid.

Beyond the Center

Set aside bulletin board or wall space to show off your children's "designer fashions"! Label the display "Meet the Pattern Pals!"

Directions

1. Use crayons to create patterns (such as stripes, checks, or polka dots) on your fabric pieces.

2. Draw the outline of a person on the sheet of paper.

3. "Dress" your person with clothes cut from the fabric pieces. Glue them in place.

Create a Border

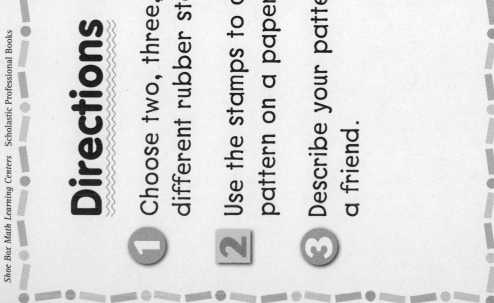

Patterns
Create a Border

Children make patterned bulletin board borders or picture frames using rubber stamps.

Materials
- shoe box
- glue
- copy of student directions
- copy of box label
- rubber stamps
- ink pads
- adding machine tape
- scissors

Putting It Together

Cut the adding machine tape into two-foot-long strips. Place the rubber stamps, ink pads, and paper strips inside the shoe box. Glue the box label to one end of the shoe box and the student directions to the inside of the lid.

Beyond the Center

Use the strips for bulletin board trimmers or frames for children's work.

Directions

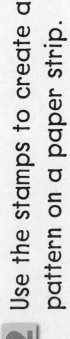

1. Choose two, three, or four different rubber stamps.

2. Use the stamps to create a pattern on a paper strip.

3. Describe your pattern to a friend.

Pattern Parade

Directions (for 4 players)

1. Deal five cards to each player. Put the remaining cards in the middle.

2. Turn over the first four cards from the pile and lay them in a row. These cards show the pattern you will repeat.

3. Take turns extending the pattern using your cards. If you don't have the card you need, pick one from the pile. If you don't pick the card you need, add it to your hand and let the next player take a turn.

4. Once the pile is gone, count up your cards. The player with the least wins.

Pattern Parade

Children extend a pattern made by the characters in a circus parade.

Materials

- shoe box
- glue
- copy of student directions
- copy of box label
- circus characters (page 42)

Putting It Together

To make two decks of cards, copy two sets of circus characters onto card stock or colored paper and cut them out. Place the cards inside the shoe box. Glue the box label to one end of the shoe box and the student directions to the inside of the lid.

Pattern Pals

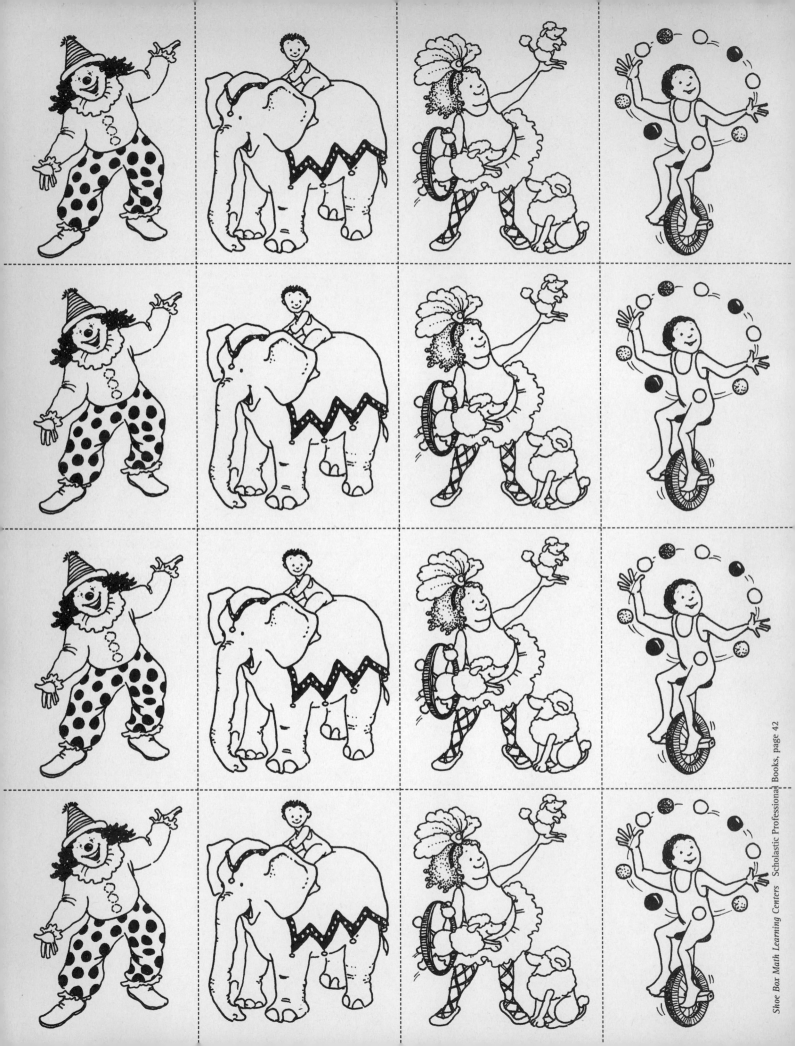

Multiplication Bingo

$6 \times 7 =$

Directions (for 2 players)

1. Take a multiplication grid and a crayon. Put two beans in the egg carton and close the carton.

2. Take turns shaking the carton and opening it. Multiply the two numbers the beans have landed on and then color in the product on your grid.

3. The first player to color in a "bingo" wins.

Multiplication Bingo

Children race to be the first to color in all the products in one row of their multiplication grid.

Materials

- shoe box
- glue
- copy of student directions
- copy of box label
- multiplication grid (page 46)
- crayons
- egg carton
- marker
- two dried beans (any type)

Putting It Together

Label the inside of each egg cup with a different number, between 0 and 10 (repeat one of the numbers on the extra cups). Make several copies of the multiplication grid. Place the egg carton, beans, grids, and crayons inside the shoe box. Glue the box label to one end of the shoe box and the student directions to the inside of the lid.

Array for Cookies!

5×2=

5×a=10

Directions

1 Choose a card.

2 Solve the problem on your card by arranging cookies on the cookie sheet.

3 Record the complete number sentence on your paper.

4 Choose a new card and repeat.

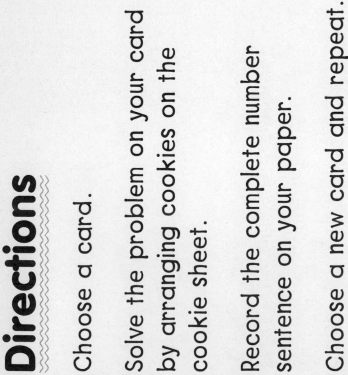

Array for Cookies!

To solve multiplication problems, children arrange cookies on a tray.

Materials

- shoe box
- glue
- copy of student directions
- copy of box label
- an assortment of small cookies or cookie-shaped cereal (stored in resealable bags)
- index cards
- markers
- copies of cookie sheet (page 47)
- paper and pencil

Putting It Together

Make several copies of the cookie sheet. Write a different multiplication problem (without the answer) on each index card. Place the cookies, index cards, and paper and pencil inside the shoe box. Glue the box label to one end of the shoe box and the student directions to the inside of the lid.

44

Picture the Facts

$6 \times 2 =$ ☐

Directions

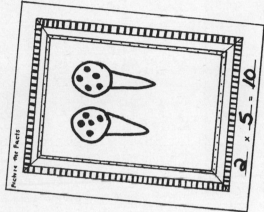

1. Choose one times table. Color these squares (for the 5's table, for example, color 5, 10, 15, 20, and so on) on the grid.

2. Based on this set, write one fact on each page of the book. Draw pictures inside each frame to show the equations. For example, for 9 × 7, you might draw 9 flowers, each with 7 petals.

Picture the Facts

Children create picture books to illustrate multiplication facts.

Materials

- shoe box
- glue
- copy of student directions
- copy of box label
- crayons
- book cover and picture frame (pages 48 and 49)
- multiplication grid (page 46)

Putting It Together

To create each book, make one copy of the cover and eleven copies of the frame and staple together. Make several copies of the multiplication grid. Place the books, crayons, and grids inside the shoe box. Glue the box label to one end of the shoe box and the student directions to the inside of the lid.

Multiplication Grid

X	0	1	2	3	4	5	6	7	8	9	10
0	0	0	0	0	0	0	0	0	0	0	0
1	0	1	2	3	4	5	6	7	8	9	10
2	0	2	4	6	8	10	12	14	16	18	20
3	0	3	6	9	12	15	18	21	24	27	30
4	0	4	8	12	16	20	24	28	32	36	40
5	0	5	10	15	20	25	30	35	40	45	50
6	0	6	12	18	24	30	36	42	48	54	60
7	0	7	14	21	28	35	42	49	56	63	70
8	0	8	16	24	32	40	48	56	64	72	80
9	0	9	18	27	36	45	54	63	72	81	90
10	0	10	20	30	40	50	60	70	80	90	100

Array for Cookies!

Picture-the-Facts Cover

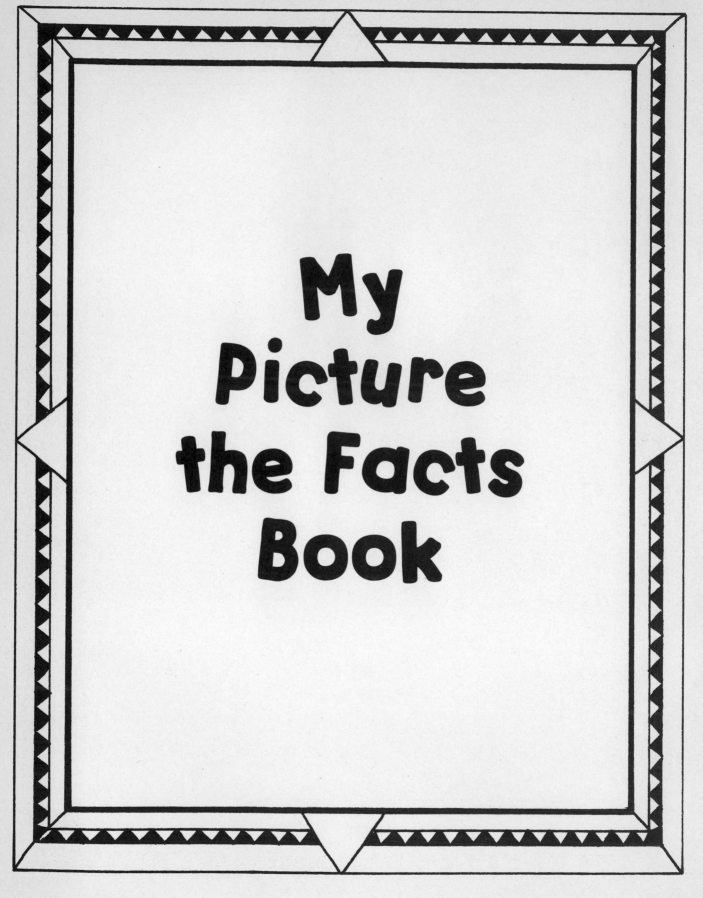

My
Picture
the Facts
Book

Name _____

Picture-the-Facts Frame

_____ X _____ = _____

Number Cube Toss

Directions

1 Guess which number will appear most often when you roll a number cube 25 times. Color in that many dots on the blank number cube at the top of your sheet.

2 Roll the number cube 25 times. Color in the squares on the graph to record your rolls.

3 Tell a classmate if your guess was correct.

Number Cube Toss

Children experiment to see which number will appear most often when a number cube is tossed 25 times.

Materials

- shoe box
- glue
- copy of student directions
- copy of box label
- number cube
- record sheet (page 53)

Putting It Together

Make several copies of the record sheet. Place the record sheets and number cube inside the shoe box. Glue the box label to one end of the shoe box and the student directions to the inside of the lid.

Beyond the Center

Combine the results from the individual graphs into a class graph by having each child color in a square to show which number he or she rolled most often.

Spin and Build

Directions

1. On your record sheet, color the block you think you might use the most of when you build your building.

2. Hold the paper clip in the center of the spinner with the pencil and spin the clip. Take a block of that color. Then color in the first square in that column.

3. Spin 24 more times. Add to your structure and your record sheet as you go.

Probability

Spin and Build

Children explore probability as they see how many blocks of each color they will use to build a structure.

Materials

- shoe box
- glue
- copy of student directions
- copy of box label
- several copies of spinner (page 55)
- crayons
- paper clips
- pencils
- record sheet (page 54)
- small interlocking blocks in different colors

Putting It Together

Copy the spinner onto card stock (have children color them according to the color words). Make several copies of the record sheet. Place the record sheets, color wheels, paper clips, pencils, and blocks inside the shoe box. Glue the box label to one end of the shoe box and the student directions to the inside of the lid.

Beyond the Center

Combine the results from the individual tally sheets into a class graph by having each child place a block on a floor graph to represent the color he or she spun most often.

Toss and Tally

Toss and Tally

Children use tally marks to record the trials of a coin toss.

Materials

- shoe box
- glue
- copy of student directions
- copy of box label
- several coins
- record sheet (page 55)
- several lunch-size paper bags

Putting It Together

Make several copies of the record sheet. Place the pennies, record sheets, and paper bags inside the shoe box. Glue the box label to one end of the shoe box and the student directions to the inside of the lid.

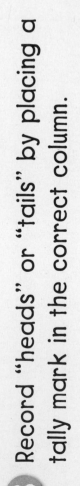

Toss and Tally Record Sheet

heads	tails
ⅢⅢ ⅢⅢ ⅢⅢ	ⅢⅢ ⅢⅢ Ⅰ

Directions

1. On your record sheet, circle the way you think the coin will land most often when tossed 25 times.

2. Put a coin inside the bag and shake it. Spill it onto the table.

3. Record "heads" or "tails" by placing a tally mark in the correct column.

4. Repeat 24 times and count the tally marks to see if your guess was right.

Number-Cube-Toss Record Sheet

I predict ☐ will be rolled most often.

Spin-and-Build Record Sheet

I predict there will be more  blocks.

red	yellow	green	blue	white	black

Spin-and-Build Spinner

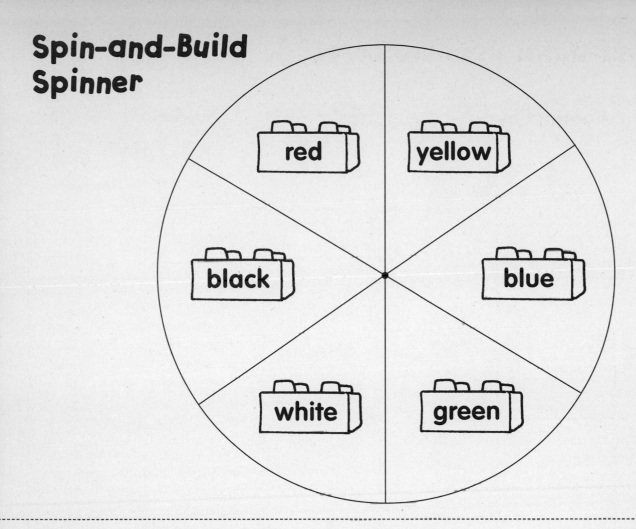

Toss-and-Tally Record Sheet

heads

tails

Clock Face Race

Children roll all the numbers needed to build a clock face.

Materials

- shoe box
- glue
- copy of student directions
- copy of box label
- clock face (page 59)
- crayons
- two number cubes

Putting It Together

Copy several clock faces onto card stock. Place the clock faces, crayons, and number cubes inside the shoe box. Glue the box label to one end of the shoe box and the student directions to the inside of the lid.

Beyond the Center

Have children cut out paper clock hands and attach them to the clock face with a brass fastener. Use for practice with telling time!

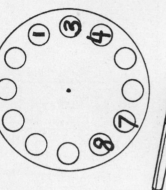

Directions (for 2 players)

1. Take turns rolling the number cubes and writing the number you rolled in the correct spot on the clock face.

2. If you roll a number you have already rolled, skip your turn.

3. The first player to complete his or her clock face wins the game.

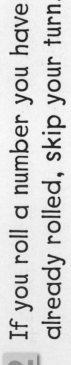

Time the Task

Directions

1. Choose one of the following tasks:
   - punch 50 holes in paper
   - stamp 50 circles on paper
   - string 50 beads
   - stack 50 blocks

2. Write your start time on the record sheet. Do the task and write the finish time.

3. Subtract the start time from the finish time to find the total time the task took.

4. Choose another task and repeat. When you finish all four tasks, circle the one that took the most time.

Time the Task

Children measure the amount of time needed to complete four tasks.

Materials

- shoe box
- glue
- copy of student directions
- copy of box label
- classroom clock or digital clock
- hole punch
- paper
- bingo daubers or markers with "stamps" at the end
- string
- beads
- interlocking blocks
- record sheet (page 59)

Putting It Together

Place the hole punch, paper, bingo daubers or markers, string, beads, interlocking blocks, and record sheets inside the shoe box. Glue the box label to one end of the shoe box and the student directions to the inside of the lid.

Grandfather Clock

Grandfather Clock

In this version of Old Maid, players avoid getting the "grandfather clock" as they match digital and analog clocks.

Materials
~~~~~~~~
- shoe box
- glue
- copy of student directions
- copy of box label
- digital clock patterns with grandfather clock card (page 60)
- analog clock patterns (page 61)

Putting It Together
~~~~~~~~
You'll need one deck of cards for each pair of students. To create a deck, make two copies of both clock sheets. Cut out all the cards. Include only one grandfather clock in the deck. Record times on each of the clocks so that each digital clock has a matching analog clock. Put the cards inside the shoe box. Glue the box label to one end of the shoe box and the student directions to the inside of the lid.

Directions (for 4 players)

1. Deal one card to each player until you run out of cards.

2. Look for matches in your hand and place them to the side. Hold the rest of the cards in your hand and take turns picking from other players to make a match. Lay down each match as you make it.

3. The player who gets rid of all of his or her cards wins. Whoever ends up with the grandfather clock at the end is "out"!

Clock Face Race

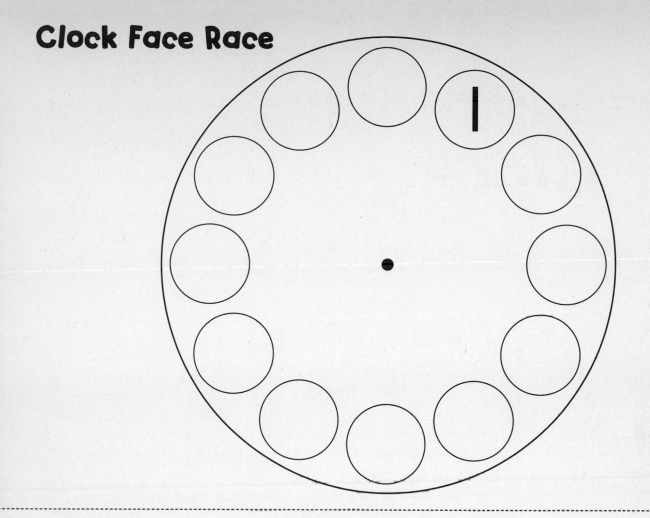

Time-the-Task Record Sheet

Task	Start Time	Finish Time	Total Task Time
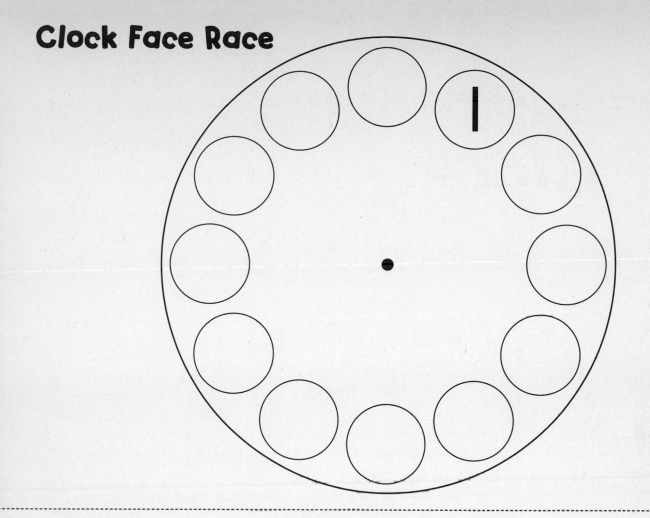			

Build the Biggest Box

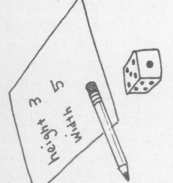

Directions (for 2 players)

1. Take turns rolling the number cubes to plan the height and width in centimeters of your box. Write the numbers on your paper.

2. Color in the squares on your grid according to the numbers you rolled.

3. Count the squares in each box to see whose is bigger. Play again using the same grid.

62

Build the Biggest Box

Children roll number cubes to determine the height and width of a box and then "construct" it on a centimeter grid.

Materials

- shoe box
- glue
- copy of student directions
- copy of box label
- centimeter grid (page 65)
- crayons
- 2 number cubes
- paper and pencil

Putting It Together

Make several copies of the centimeter grid. Place the grids, crayons, and number cubes inside the shoe box. Glue the box label to one end of the shoe box and the student directions to the inside of the lid.

Estimate and Weigh

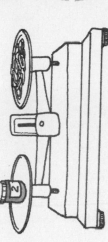

Directions

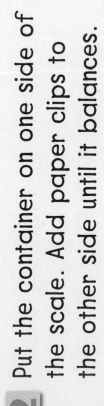

1 Choose a container. Estimate the weight of the container in paper clips and write it on the record sheet.

2 Put the container on one side of the scale. Add paper clips to the other side until it balances.

3 Write down the weight of the container in paper clips. Repeat using different containers.

Estimate and Weigh

Children estimate and weigh film canisters filled with various items.

Materials

- shoe box
- glue
- copy of student directions
- copy of box label
- 8 film canisters each filled with a different material (pebbles, bird seed, sand, salt, rice, dried pasta, cereal, and beans)
- masking tape
- box of paper clips
- balance scale(s)
- record sheet (page 65)

Putting It Together

Make several copies of the record sheet. Use masking tape to label each film canister with a number between 1 and 8. Place the film canisters, paper clips, and record sheets inside the shoe box. Set up the balance scale(s) at the center. Glue the box label to one end of the shoe box and the student directions to the inside of the lid.

Building a House

Directions

1. Choose a house plan.

2. On your paper, draw a house using your ruler and the measurements of the plans. Draw the house part first and then add everything else.

3. Decorate your house with crayons or markers.

Building a House

Children follow blueprints to draw a house to scale.

Materials

- shoe box
- glue
- copy of student directions
- copy of box label
- house plans (page 66)
- rulers
- paper
- crayons or markers

Putting It Together

Copy the house plans onto card stock and cut them out. Place the plans, rulers, paper, and crayons or markers inside the shoe box. Glue the box label to one end of the shoe box and the student directions to the inside of the lid.

Beyond the Center

For an even greater challenge, let children use the house plans to build 3-D models from cardboard.

Build the Biggest Box Grid

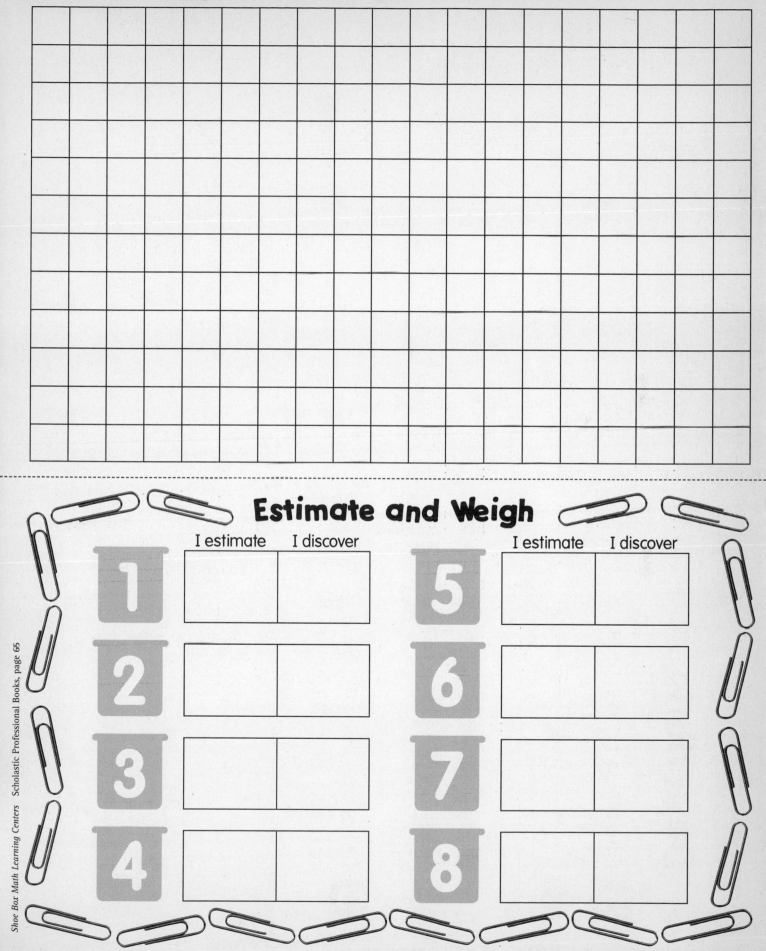

Estimate and Weigh

	I estimate	I discover		I estimate	I discover
1			**5**		
2			**6**		
3			**7**		
4			**8**		

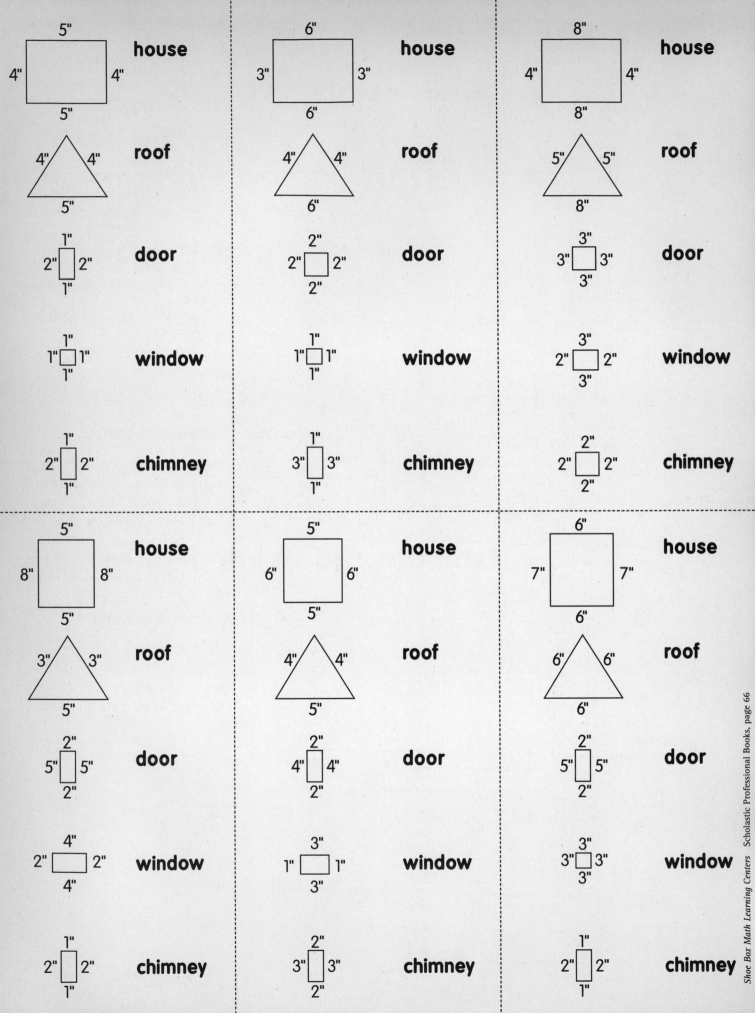

house · roof · door · window · chimney

Money in the Bank

Children create unique piggy banks and add up their contents.

Materials

- shoe box
- glue
- copy of student directions
- copy of box label
- large handful of coins
- crayons
- piggy bank pattern (page 70)

Putting It Together

Make several copies of the piggy bank pattern on pink paper. Place the piggy banks, coins, and crayons inside the shoe box. Glue the box label to one end of the shoe box and the student directions to the inside of the lid.

Beyond the Center

Have children trade piggy banks before adding up their coins, and instead, add up the contents of each other's banks.

Directions

1. Choose some coins and place them under the piggy bank.

2. Use the crayons to make a rubbing of each coin.

3. Add up the coins and write the total at the bottom of your bank.

Count Your Change

Directions

1. Choose two change purses. Write their numbers on the purses in the first row of the record sheet.

2. Count the value of the coins in each purse. Write the amounts on your sheet.

3. Circle the purse that held the most money.

4. Choose two more purses and repeat.

Count Your Change

Children count and compare the value of two sets of coins.

Materials

- shoe box
- glue
- copy of student directions
- copy of box label
- an assortment of coins
- 10 change purses and/or wallets
- record sheet (page 70)
- pencils

Putting It Together

Fill each change purse with a different amount of coins. Label each purse with a number between 1 and 10. Make several copies of the record sheet. Place the change purses and record sheets inside the shoe box. Glue the box label to one end of the shoe box and the student directions to the inside of the lid.

Shoe Box Math Learning Centers Scholastic Professional Books

Race for a Dollar

Race for a Dollar

Children trade coins in a race to be the first to trade their change for a dollar.

Materials

- shoe box
- glue
- copy of student directions
- copy of box label
- game board (page 71)
- number cubes
- coins
- one dollar bill

Putting It Together

Make copies of the game board. Place the game boards, number cubes, and coins inside the shoe box. Glue the box label to one end of the shoe box and the student directions to the inside of the lid.

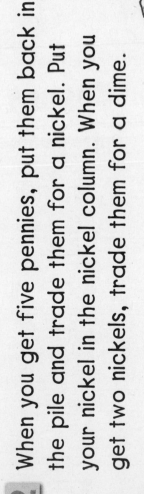

Directions

1 Each player gets a gameboard. Put all the coins in a pile. Take turns rolling the number cube and placing that number of pennies on the penny shapes on your game board.

2 When you get five pennies, put them back in the pile and trade them for a nickel. Put your nickel in the nickel column. When you get two nickels, trade them for a dime.

3 The first player to get ten dimes and trade them for one dollar wins!

Money in the Bank

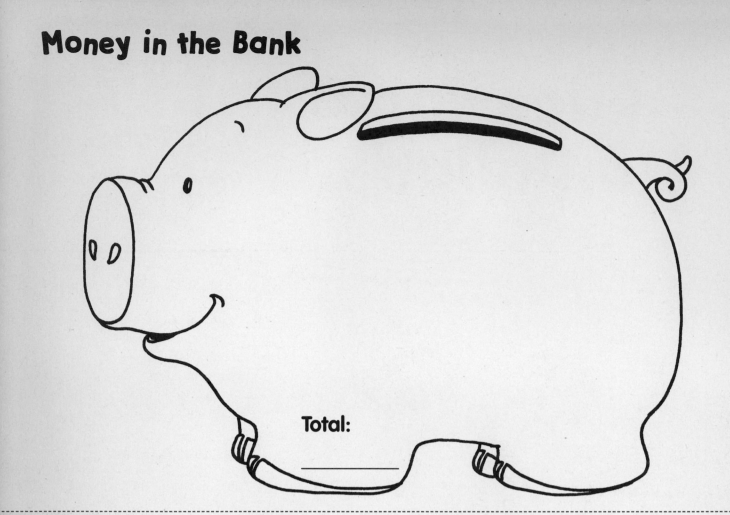

Total:

_____

Count Your Change

Purse Number	Amount	Purse Number	Amount
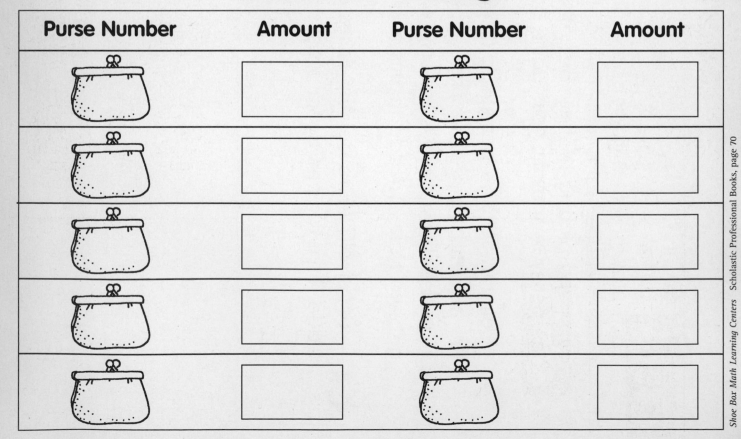			

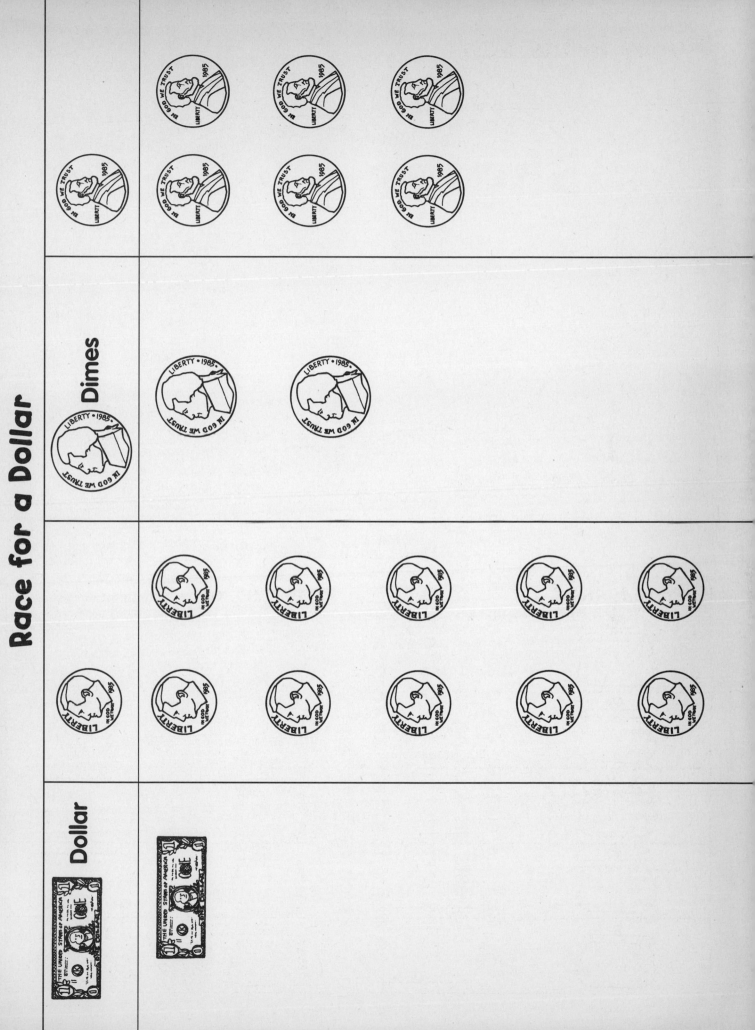

Race for a Dollar

Dollar

Dimes

Fair Shares

Children create food from playdough and slice it into equal parts.

Materials

- shoe box
- glue
- copy of student directions
- copy of box label
- playdough
- plastic knives
- food cards (page 76)
- number cube

Putting It Together

Copy the food cards onto card stock. Place the cards, playdough, plastic knives, and number cube inside the shoe box. Glue the box label to one end of the shoe box and the student directions to the inside of the lid.

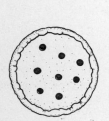

Directions

1. Choose a food card. Make the food from playdough.

2. Roll the number cube to see how many guests are coming to eat. Based on that number, cut the food into equal parts.

3. Name the fraction for each part (such as $\frac{1}{3}, \frac{1}{3}, \frac{1}{3}$).

How Old Are You Now?

Directions

1 Choose a bag.

2 Divide the candles evenly among the cakes.

3 Choose another bag and repeat.

How Old Are You Now?

Children divide candles evenly among birthday cakes.

Materials

- shoe box
- glue
- copy of student directions
- copy of box label
- cake patterns (page 77)
- 170 birthday candles
- construction paper
- eight large resealable plastic bags

Putting It Together

Copy 44 cakes onto construction paper and cut them out. In eight bags, place the following sets:

2 cakes and 12 candles
3 cakes and 12 candles
4 cakes and 16 candles
5 cakes and 25 candles
6 cakes and 24 candles
7 cakes and 14 candles
8 cakes and 40 candles
9 cakes and 27 candles

Place the bags inside the shoe box. Glue the box label to one end of the shoe box and the student directions to the inside of the lid.

Roll a Fraction

Children complete pies by coloring in fractional amounts.

Materials

- shoe box
- glue
- copy of student directions
- copy of box label
- game board (page 77)
- crayons
- two number cubes

Putting It Together

Make several copies of the game board. Place the game boards, number cubes and crayons inside the shoe box. Glue the box label to one end of the shoe box and the student directions to the inside of the lid.

Directions

1. Take turns rolling the number cubes and making fractions from the two numbers. For example, if you roll 2 and 3, the fraction is $\frac{2}{3}$.

2. Based on that fraction, color in pie slices on your game board. For $\frac{2}{3}$, you would color in two slices of the pie cut in thirds.

3. As you play, color in all available slices. The first player to color in all of the slices on all of the pies wins!

Silly Soup

Silly Soup

To make "Silly Soup," children follow a recipe and measure the ingredients in fractional amounts.

Materials

- shoe box
- glue
- copy of student directions
- copy of box label
- recipe cards (page 78)
- dried pasta
- dried rice
- dried beans
- popcorn
- cereal
- five resealable plastic bags
- large bowl
- spoon
- small measuring cups
- measuring pitcher

Putting It Together

Place each ingredient (pasta, rice, and so on) in a separate resealable plastic bag. Make copies of the recipe cards. Place the bags, recipe cards, spoon, and measuring cups inside the shoe box. Glue the box label to one end of the shoe box and the student directions to the inside of the lid.

TIP

To reuse the materials, let students sort the ingredients and place them back in the bags at the end of the day.

Directions

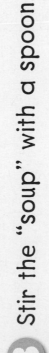
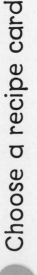

1 Choose a recipe card.

2 Measure each ingredient. Pour it into the bowl.

3 Stir the "soup" with a spoon.

4 Find out how much "soup" you've made by pouring it from the bowl into the measuring pitcher.

How Old Are You Now?

Roll a Fraction

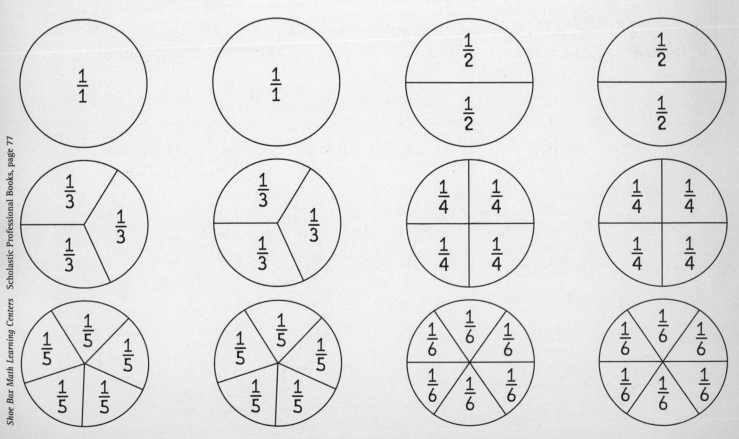

Silly Soup

Silly Soup Recipe 1

Ingredients:

$\frac{1}{2}$ cup pasta

$\frac{2}{3}$ cup rice

$\frac{3}{4}$ cup beans

1 cup popcorn

$\frac{1}{3}$ cup cereal

Mix well and serve!

Silly Soup Recipe 2

Ingredients:

1 cup pasta

$\frac{1}{2}$ cup rice

$\frac{1}{3}$ cup beans

$\frac{1}{3}$ cup popcorn

1 cup cereal

Mix well and serve!

Silly Soup Recipe 3

Ingredients:

$\frac{2}{3}$ cup pasta

$\frac{1}{3}$ cup rice

$\frac{1}{4}$ cup beans

$\frac{1}{4}$ cup popcorn

$\frac{1}{4}$ cup cereal

Mix well and serve!

Silly Soup Recipe 4

Ingredients:

$\frac{1}{4}$ cup pasta

1 cup rice

$\frac{1}{3}$ cup beans

$\frac{2}{3}$ cup popcorn

1 cup cereal

Mix well and serve!

Silly Soup Recipe 5

Ingredients:

$\frac{2}{3}$ cup pasta

$\frac{1}{3}$ cup rice

$\frac{2}{3}$ cup beans

1 cup popcorn

1 cup cereal

Mix well and serve!

Silly Soup Recipe 6

Ingredients:

$\frac{1}{2}$ cup pasta

$\frac{1}{3}$ cup rice

$\frac{1}{3}$ cup beans

$\frac{1}{3}$ cup popcorn

$\frac{1}{3}$ cup cereal

Mix well and serve!

Silly Soup Recipe 7

Ingredients:

$\frac{2}{3}$ cup pasta

$\frac{1}{3}$ cup rice

1 cup beans

1 cup popcorn

1 cup cereal

Mix well and serve!

Silly Soup Recipe 8

Ingredients:

$\frac{1}{3}$ cup pasta

1 cup rice

$\frac{1}{3}$ cup beans

$\frac{2}{3}$ cup popcorn

$\frac{2}{3}$ cup cereal

Mix well and serve!

Silly Soup Recipe 9

Ingredients:

$\frac{1}{2}$ cup pasta

$\frac{2}{3}$ cup rice

$\frac{1}{4}$ cup beans

$\frac{3}{4}$ cup popcorn

$\frac{1}{3}$ cup cereal

Mix well and serve!

Notes

Notes